YOU DON'T DEFINE ME
I DEFINE MYSELF
WORKBOOK

EXCERCISES AND PRACTICES TO HELP YOU DEFINE YOURSELF

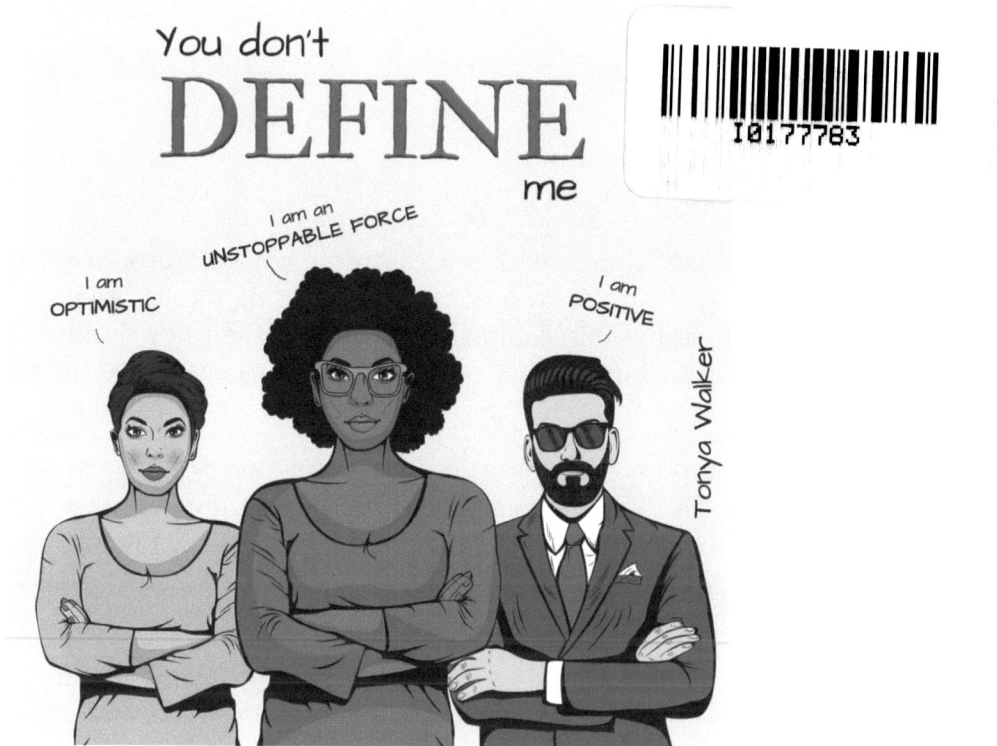

You don't
DEFINE
me

I am an
UNSTOPPABLE FORCE

I am
OPTIMISTIC

I am
POSITIVE

Tonya Walker

New Life Portfolio
Create the life you want opposed to the life that someone else wants

Begin Again
Discover the gifts and talents within

The New You
Let us go on a journey that will change your life forever
and

Define Yourself

Written and Created by Tonya Walker

RENEWED MIND

EXERCISES TO KEEP YOUR MIND RENEWED

YOU DON'T DEFINE ME

I DEFINE MYSELF

Our mission is to help people to redefine their life by bringing awareness of what is on the inside of them

GOALS

1. Motivate people through positive change

2. Boost self-esteem and self-confidence through positive affirmations

3. Promoting the social growth of people so that they can thrive and succeed in life

4. Teach people to believe in themselves

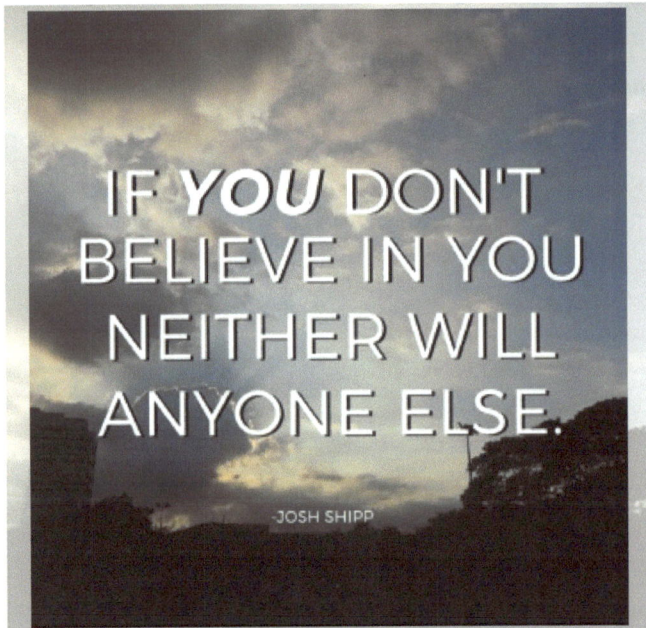

IF **YOU** DON'T BELIEVE IN YOU NEITHER WILL ANYONE ELSE.

-JOSH SHIPP

STEPS

1. Discover where you are in life

2. Make goals to help accomplish your vision

3. Create steps to accomplish your goals

4. Create habits around your steps

LIFE ASSESSMENT

And the Lord answered me, and said: "Write the vision, and make it plain upon tables, that he may run that readeth it. For the vision is yet for an appointed time, but at the end it shall speak, and not lie: though it tarry, wait for it; because it will surely come, it will not tarry."

Habakkuk 2:2 & 3

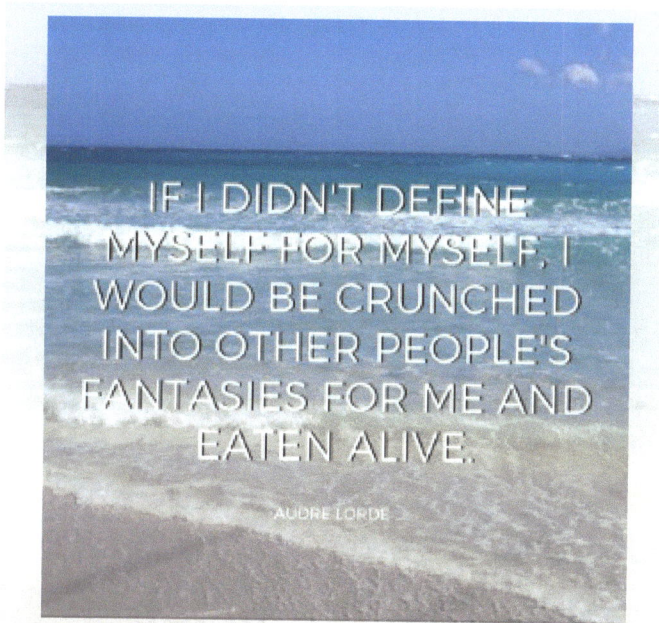

IF I DIDN'T DEFINE MYSELF FOR MYSELF, I WOULD BE CRUNCHED INTO OTHER PEOPLE'S FANTASIES FOR ME AND EATEN ALIVE.

AUDRE LORDE

Write down 3 issues that you want to see improved in each area. On the first line, write the issue. Write a positive word on line 1 (the opposite of the issue). Create a positive affirmation on line 2 for the area that you can repeat daily.

Health

1. _____

    1. _____

    2. _____

2. _____

1. _____

2. _____

3. _____

   1. _____

   2. _____

Family and Friends

1. _____

   1. _____

   2. _____

2. _____

   1. _____

   2. _____

3. _____

   1. _____

   2. _____

Love Relationship

1. _____

   1. _____

   2. _____

2. _____

   1. _____

2. _____

3. _____

   1. _____

   2. _____

And the Lord answered me, and said, Write the vision, and make it plain upon tables, that he may run that readeth it. For the vision is yet for an appointed time, but at the end it shall speak, and not lie: though it tarry, wait for it; because it will surely come, it will not tarry.

Habakkuk 2:2 & 3

Entrepreneur/Employment

1. _____

   1. _____

   2. _____

2. _____

   1. _____

   2. _____

3. _____

   1. _____

   2. _____

Finances

1. _____

   1. _____

2. _____

2. _____

    1. _____

    2. _____

3. _____

    1. _____

    2. _____

Parenting

1. _____

    1. _____

    2. _____

2. _____

    1. _____

    2. _____

3. _____

    1. _____

    2. _____

And the Lord answered me, and said, Write the vision, and make it plain upon tables, that he may run that readeth it. For the vision is yet for an appointed time, but at the end it shall speak, and not lie: though it tarry, wait for it; because it will surely come, it will not tarry.

Habakkuk 2:2 & 3

Spirituality

1. _____ _____

    1. _____

    2. _____

2. _____

    1. _____

    2. _____

3. _____

    1. _____

    2. _____

Education

1. _____

    1. _____

    2. _____

2. _____

    1. _____

    2. _____

3. _____

    1. _____

    2. _____

CREATE YOUR VISION

"A Man without a vision for his future will always return to his past"

- Bishop Lalachan Abraham

Write a vision for your life and then create a vision board.

Dear Vision,

_____

_____

_____

_____

_____

_____

_____

_____

_____

_____

_____

_____

And the Lord answered me, and said, Write the vision, and make it plain upon tables, that he may run that readeth it. For the vision is yet for an appointed time, but at the end it shall speak, and not lie: though it tarry, wait for it; because it will surely come, it will not tarry.

Habakkuk 2:2 & 3

CREATING AFFIRMATIONS

Write positive quotes about yourself in the space below

I CAN DO ANYTHING!
I FULLY TRUST AND BELIEVE IN MYSELF.

1. _____
2. _____
3. _____
4. _____
5. _____
6. _____
7. _____
8. _____
9. _____
10. _____
11. _____
12. _____

NO ONE WILL BELIEVE IN YOU - UNLESS YOU BELIEVE IN YOURSELF FIRST

What Beliefs Do You Have About Yourself? What Beliefs Should You Have About Yourself to Accomplish Your Goals?

Write down negative things in the first column that you have been told over the years. In the second column write down the positive version and focus on that side alone.

1. _____   1. _____

2. _____   2. _____

3. _____   3. _____

4. _____   4. _____

5. _____   5. _____

6. _____   6. _____

7. _____   7. _____

8. _____   8. _____

9. _____   9. _____

10. _____   10. _____

11. _____   11. _____

12. _____   12. _____

13. _____   13. _____

14. _____   14. _____

15. _____   15. _____

16. _____   16. _____

17. _____   17. _____

18. _____   18. _____

19. _____   19. _____

20. _____   20. _____

21. _____   21. _____

22. _____   22. _____

And all things, whatsoever ye shall ask in prayer, believing, ye shall receive.

Matthew 21:22

IT IS TIME TO GET OUT OF THE BUCKET

YOU ARE CREATED IN THE IMAGE OF GOD

What has your foundation been built on? Let us build our foundation to ensure that it is solid.

Learn To Use Faith to Activate That Which the Father Deposited Within You

Life is what you create it to be. If you have a fragile foundation your hopes and dreams will shatter when you begin adding layers. If you have a solid foundation your hopes, dreams, will surely manifest.

Start today by building a solid foundation.

Start with declaring your positive quotes and positive affirmations. Every time you are approached with any type of negativity, repeat the positive quotes and affirmations.

Start working on yourself daily for 15 minutes a day by listening to positive videos or reading a positive book.

21 DAY FAST

What are you willing to give up to live your dream? Go on a 21 day fast. On each line list something that you will give up each day for the next 21 days.

1. _____

2, _____

3. _____

4. _____

5. _____

6. _____

7. _____

8. _____

9. _____

10. _____

11. _____

12. _____

13. _____

14. _____

15. _____

16. _____

17. _____

18. _____

19. _____

20. _____

21. _____

GO BEYOND THE NATURAL

Wake up early every morning to set-up your day! Make a list of things that need to be done daily to be the best version of yourself.

1. _____

_____

2. _____

_____

3. _____

_____

4. _____

_____

5. _____

_____

6. _____

_____

7. _____

_____

8. _____

_____

9. _____

_____

10. _____

_____

THE STOP/START PRINCIPLE

What do you need to stop doing and start doing to fulfill your dreams?
Make a list of goals and try to reach them. Record your progress.

1. _____
2. _____
3. _____
4. _____
5. _____
6. _____
7. _____
8. _____
9. _____
10. _____
11. _____
12. _____
13. _____
14. _____
15. _____
16. _____
17. _____
18. _____
19. _____
20. _____

GOD WILL DO A NEW THING THIS YEAR

Behold, I will do a new thing; now it shall spring forth; shall ye not know it? I will even make a way in the wilderness, and rivers in the desert.

Isaiah 43:19 KJV.......

- Write down 5 of your biggest success moments
- Write down 5 highlights of your day
- Write down 5 of your best decisions today

Successes

1. _____

2. _____

3. _____

4. _____

5. _____

Highlights

1. _____

2. _____

3. _____

4. _____

5. _____

Decisions

1. _____

2. _____

3. _____

4. _____

5. _____

"No weapon formed against you shall prosper, And every tongue which rises against you in judgment. You shall condemn. This is the heritage of the servants of the Lord. And their righteousness is from Me," Says the Lord!

MENTORS

You might be in a situation or environment that leaves you without a mentor, but everyone has access to books.

When you read a book – it is like spending time with that author.

Let the author be your mentor.

Book Suggestions

1. As a Man Thinketh – James Allen
2. The Charge – Brendon Burchard
3. Mandela's Way – Richard Stengel
4. The Power of Awareness – Neville Goddard
5. Instinct – TD Jakes
6. How to Win Friends and Influence People – Dale Carnegie
7. The 15 Invaluable Laws of Growth – John C Maxwell
8. Think and Grow Rich – Napoleon Hill
9. Rich Dad Poor Dad – Robert Kiyosaki
10. The Richest Man in Babylon – Napoleon Hill Foundation
11. Hung by the Tongue - Francis P Martin
12. You Don't Define Me - Tonya Walker
13. The Power of Positive Thinking - Norman Vincent Peale
14. Man's Search for Meaning - Viktor E. Frankl
15. Success Through A Positive Mental Attitude - Napoleon Hill
16. Don't Sweat the Small Stuff - Richard Carlson

MODELING

Research who is successful at doing what you want to do. Write down three things that you found that will help you accomplish your goals.

1. _____

2. _____

3. _____

After your research is complete – Take Action

ACTION STEPS

1. Listen to What they are Saying – Let it Soak in by Mediating on it Daily

2. Create a Vision for What You Want To Achieve

3. Set Your Mind on the Finish Product

4. Create Affirmations to Speak Daily about the Finished Product

5. Set Small Goals Weekly to Work on your Vision

6. Set Steps to Accomplish your Goals Weekly

7. Create Strong Habits around Your Vision

8. Set a Deadline

9. Visualize the Finished Product Daily

10. At the End of Each Day Create a Heart of Gratitude

11. Don't Tell People until It's Complete Unless They Are Helping You!

But thou, when thou prayest, enter into thy closet, and when thou hast shut thy door, pray to thy Father which is in secret; and thy Father which seeth in secret shall reward thee openly.

Matthew 6:6

COLLABORATE YOUR MIND

I want this – I chose this – I have chosen to love this

Follow the example below and write down what you want, choose, and have chosen to love.

Example:

1.   I want to write – I have chosen to write – I love writing – I can take the pain of discipline to write – I'm the best – I'm the greatest – I am an expert at writing # 1 New York Best Selling Books & International books in several different languages.

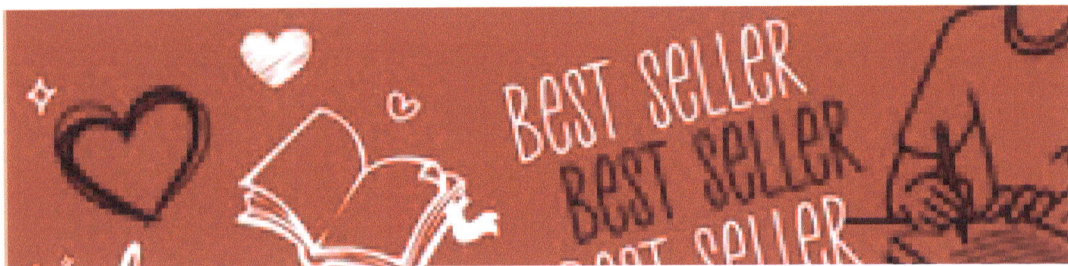

2.   _____

_____

_____

_____

3.   _____

_____

_____

_____

MIND EXERCISE

Everyone Works on the Body, but who Works on the Mind

Ways to Open your Mind

1. Go for a walk

2. Write down your thoughts in a journal

3. Read a book

4. Meditate – Breathe deep for one minute

5. Seek a quiet place for three minutes and sit

6. Go to the gym

7. Talk to a friend

8. Repeat a positive quote over and over again

MUSIC IS A GREAT WAY TO FEEL AND VISUALIZE YOUR DREAMS

Everyone Works on the Body, but who Work on the Mind

Ways to Open your Mind

1. Create a song from your *Life Assessment Worksheet*

2. Write the song as if it is already created & write it as if you really love and want it

3. Put Music to the words

4. Create a Powerpoint presentation to go along with your song

CREATE A SONG
SING THE SONG
GET IT IN YOUR SPIRIT

Examples on the following pages

I AM HEALTHY SONG

I love to exercise – I chose to walk three times a week for 30 minutes – I chose to dance for 20 minutes 3 days a week

I want to exercise – I want to exercise – I choose to exercise – I choose to exercise - I love to exercise - I love to exercise – I want it – I want it – I really, really want it - I really, really want it

I love to eat vegetables three times a day – I chose to juice vegetables daily – I choose to eat vegetables with every meal

I want to eat vegetables – I want to eat vegetables – I choose to eat vegetables – I choose to eat vegetables - I love to eat vegetables - I love to eat vegetables – I want it – I want it – I really, really want it - I really, really want it

I love to practice a healthy mindset – I chose to speak health affirmations daily –I chose to visualize myself healthy daily

I want to practice a healthy mindset – I want to practice a healthy mindset – I choose to practice a healthy mindset – I choose to practice a healthy mindset - I love to practice a healthy mindset - I love to practice a healthy mindset – I want it – I want it – I really, really want it - I really, really want it

I am healthy - I am healthy - I am healthy - I am healthy - I am healthy
I am healthy - I am healthy - I am healthy - I am healthy - I am healthy
I am healthy - I am healthy - I am healthy - I am healthy - I am healthy

I AM SUCCESSFUL SONG

I love to write my book – I chose to write thirty minutes daily – I chose to read books on writing

I want to write my book – I want to write my book – I choose to write my book – I choose to write my book - I love to write my book - I love to write my book – I want it – I want it – I really, really want it - I really, really want it

I love to develop programs & create workshops – I choose to study other successful programs – I chose to visualize my program & workshop complete & successful

I want to develop programs & create workshops – I want to develop programs & create workshops – I choose to develop programs & create workshops – I choose to develop programs & create workshops - I love to develop programs & create workshops - I love to develop programs & create workshops – I want it – I want it – I really, really want it - I really, really want it

I love to visualize my book complete – I choose to meditate & see the mission complete – I chose to speak affirmations daily about my mission

I want to visualize my book complete – I want to visualize my book complete – I choose to visualize my book complete – I choose to visualize my book complete - I love to visualize my book complete - I love to visualize my book complete – I want it – I want it – I really, really want it - I really, really want it

I am manifesting my mission - I am manifesting my mission
I am manifesting my mission - I am manifesting my mission
I am manifesting my mission - I am manifesting my mission
I am manifesting my mission - I am manifesting my mission
I am manifesting my mission - I am manifesting my mission

I AM WEALTHY SONG

I love to pay my tithe – I chose to speak affirmations about tithe – I chose to give with a joyful heart

I want to pay my tithe – I want to pay my tithe – I choose to pay my tithe – I choose to pay my tithe - I love to pay my tithe - I love to pay my tithe – I want it – I want it – I really, really want it - I really, really want it

I love to pay myself – I chose to pay myself $2000.00 a week – I chose to read books about investing

I want to pay myself – I want to pay myself – I choose to pay myself – I choose to pay myself - I love to pay myself - I love to pay myself – I want it – I want it – I really, really want it - I really, really want it

I love to learn from others that are successful in finances – I chose to speak that I am debt-free – I choose to read books & look at videos

I want to learn from others that are successful in finances – I want to learn from others that are successful in finances – I choose to learn from others that are success-ful in finances – I choose to learn from others that are successful in finances - I love to learn from others that are successful in finances - I love to learn from others that are successful in finances – I want it – I want it – I really, really want it - I really, really want it

**I am wealthy - I am wealthy - I am wealthy - I am wealthy - I am wealthy
I am wealthy - I am wealthy - I am wealthy - I am wealthy - I am wealthy
I am wealthy - I am wealthy - I am wealthy - I am wealthy - I am wealthy**

CREATE A SONG ABOUT YOUR LIFE

_____

_____

_____

_____

_____

_____

_____

_____

_____

_____

_____

_____

_____

_____

_____

_____

_____

_____

WHAT ARE YOU GRATEFUL FOR?

List three things daily that you are grateful for in life.

Monday
1. _____
2. _____
3. _____

Tuesday
1. _____
2. _____
3. _____

Wednesday
1. _____
2. _____
3. _____

Thursday
1. _____
2. _____
3. _____

Friday

1. _____

2. _____

3. _____

Saturday

1. _____

2. _____

3. _____

Sunday

1. _____

2. _____

3. _____

MAKE A LIST OF PEOPLE AND THEIR NEEDS TO PRAY FOR DAILY

Let each of you look not only to his own interests, but also to the interest of others.

Philippians 2:4

Praying for someone is definitely a great way to help someone. List people in need and commit to pray daily for them.

1. _____

2. _____

3. _____

4. _____

5. _____

6. _____

7. _____

8. _____

9. _____

10. _____

WHAT PATH WILL YOU TAKE?

1. Draw a Picture of a Path Going in Three Different Directions

2. Name the Different Road Blocks on One Path

3. On the Second Path Put What Everyone Else Wants You to Do

4. On the Last Path Go Straight to Your Destination

5. Choose What You Will Carry on Your Journey

WAYS TO STRENGTHEN YOUR SKILLS

If you Don't Have the Skill – Create It

How Bad Do You Want It

Create a list of skills that you believe you do very well and ways to strengthen it.

1. _____

2. _____

3. _____

4. _____

5. _____

6. _____

7. _____

1. Create it 2. Practice it 3. Make it a Habit 4. Master it

Create a list of skills that you would love to have and ways to strengthen it.

1. _____

2. _____

3. _____

4. _____

5. _____

6. _____

7. _____

1. Create it 2. Practice it 3. Make it a Habit 4. Master it

Ways to Strengthen your Skills

If you Don't Have the Skill – Create It

How Bad Do You Want It

Create a list of skills that you would love to have and ways to strengthen it.

1. _____

2. _____

3. _____

4. _____

5. _____

6. _____

7. _____

1. Create it 2. Practice it 3. Make it a Habit 4. Master it

WRITE YOURSELF A LETTER

DESCRIBE ALL THE GOOD THINGS THAT YOU HAVE DONE AND PLAN ON DOING

Write it as if it has Already Taken Place

Read this Letter Every Time You Feel Down

Example

Dear ....,

I am...

I love..about myself.......................................

I feel...

Sincerely, ...

......and calleth those things which are not, as though they were

Romans 4:17

Dear _____,

_____

_____

_____

_____

_____

_____

_____

_____

_____

_____

_____

_____

_____

_____

_____

_____

_____

Sincerely, _____

LET'S LEAP AND GROW OUR WINGS ON THE WAY DOWN

What can you do to Start Living your Dreams Now?

Whatever is in your hand – use it!

Write it down below! (For example, sign up for a class) Start acting on it today!

1. _____

2. _____

3. _____

4. _____

5. _____

6. _____

Declaring the end from the beginning….

Isaiah 46:10

THINGS I ACCOMPLISHED IN LIFE

Write Down Everything You Plan to Achieve in Life

Create a Vision Board to Reflect

Start Declaring and Decreeing

_____

_____

_____

_____

_____

_____

_____

_____

_____

_____

_____

_____

Declaring the end from the beginning…

Isaiah 46:10

NOTES

www.ingramcontent.com/pod-product-compliance
Lightning Source LLC
Chambersburg PA
CBHW040024050426

42452CB00003B/132